# Successfully Litigating (And Winning) Personal Injury Cases In Virginia

## Don't Be A Victim… Fight Back

By O. Keith Hallam, Jr., Esq.

**ISBN:** 978-1-941645-28-4

**Design and Published by:**

**Speakeasy Publications**

73-03 Bell Blvd #10

Oakland Gardens, N.Y. 11364

www.SpeakeasyMarketingInc.com

888-225-8594

# DISCLAIMER

This publication is intended to be informational only. No legal advice is being given, and no attorney-client relationship is intended to be created by reading this material. If you are facing legal issues, whether criminal or civil, seek professional legal counsel to get your questions answered.

**NovaLegalGroup, P.C.**

1507 King Street

Alexandria, VA 22314

(703) 548-1462

www.NovaLegalGroup.com

# Client Testimonials

*"I highly recommend Attorney O. Keith Hallam Jr. and his dedicated staff. Mr. Hallam helped me on two separate occasions regarding vehicle accidents I had been involved in. Both times I was not at fault but the other insurance companies did not want to cover all of the medical bills nor the cost of being out of work while recovering. Mr. Hallam was able to get them to cover all of my expenses, along with extra for my long-term pain and suffering. Had I not hired Mr. Hallam, only my vehicle would've been repaired, not my bodily injuries and ensuing bills. Thanks Mr. Hallam!"*

**- Automobile Accident Client**

........................................................................

*"I am more than grateful that Mr. Hallam and his colleagues were able to help me with my case. I was facing a DUI with a BAC greater than .20, and I was involved in an accident. He fought for me and had my back the whole way. When it came down to my trial everything was dismissed by the grace of God, I am truly blessed. I recently recommended one of my friends to his office. Im for certain that he will fight for them the same way he fought for me. He let me know the brutal truth*

*about my case and didn't give me false hope. I will forever be thankful for what Mr. Hallam did for me. And I will always recommend him to anyone who is looking for an attorney. Thank you all so much for all of your help, I am beyond grateful."* **- Diamond**

........................................................................................

*"Wanted to express how amazing my treatment was with Keith and his associates. He jumped on my case immediately. Got things resolved very affordably and in a timely manner without the run around I have received with prior counsel. Followed up with me after my court date which I felt was wonderful. Keith and his team are professional, prompt, and worked quickly to resolve my case. I would highly recommend Keith for your next attorney. Everything from the person receiving the calls to returning my calls was handled professionally. I would definitely choose Keith again in the future."*

**- Todd**

........................................................................................

# TABLE OF CONTENTS

# About The Author

O. Keith Hallam, Jr. has practiced Criminal Traffic Law, Criminal Law and Personal Injury/Accident Law for nearly 30 years – successfully representing over 10,000+ clients during this time, throughout all the courts of Northern Virginia and many other courts throughout all of Virginia. Mr. Hallam is well-known throughout this area as being one of the first, if not the first attorney, to design customized "Plans of Action" for he and his clients to pursue together, requiring that both he and his clients work as a "team," together to successfully defend and win their cases.

Mr. Hallam's customized "Plans of Action" are designed so that both the attorney and the client have well-defined, due diligence actions and "homework" to perform proactively before court, so as to determine and find "holes" in the prosecution's case and for the client to engage in certain actions and take certain classes before court, such as various "Driver Improvement" classes; alcohol education classes; community service and letters of recommendations, all to place the client in the most favorable light possible when the attorney must try the DUI case or work to negotiate a favorable reduction or dismissal of the DUI charge with the prosecutor.

Mr. Hallam has also been one of the first attorneys in Northern Virginia to put trust and confidence in his clients, as they do him by designing customized "Payment Plans" to fit each client's unique financial situation.

## SUCCESSFULLY DEFENDING (AND WINNING) DUI CASES IN VIRGINIA!

**Don't Be A Victim..... Fight Back!**

# WHY DO YOU HANDLE PERSONAL INJURY CASES?

There is a saying that, "Other cases pay the rent, but personal injury cases pay for the vacation home." While this may sound mercenary, it is true. In handling personal injury cases, attorneys want to add value for their clients and clients come first, but you are not being honest with yourself or your clients if it's not immediately understood that, while you're in business to help yourself and your firm, you are first and foremost in business to help your clients. If you can do both, then it's a win-win for everyone.

In personal injury law, we add value for our clients, in that we don't just handle a case against another person or business that hurt them, but also to work to get them the best medical care available. Most personal injury lawyers don't do that; they take their clients as they come, they handle the submission of a claim and negotiate a settlement or trial and demand and or get compensation for injuries but they don't get involved with the client's personal needs the way we do.

We are associated with an outstanding group of doctors and physical therapists in the Northern Virginia area; most are board certified, and they have agreed to accept our referrals, so that clients who need additional medical help, but who don't have health insurance or the resources or knowledge to know how to do so can get the treatment they need. We provide these referrals and recommendations to physicians, physical therapists, chiropractors and others in the field and they will treat our clients for as long as necessary to make sure they reach maximum medical improvement without charging them one penny before, during or after their treatment; they will wait until the case is complete to be paid from the settlement proceeds.

The value and beauty of this is that, in most of the cases we've handled, we have gotten many people the medical care they needed, but couldn't have accessed or afforded before; by referring them to healthcare providers for absolutely no cost upfront or during the treatment, and this is a service we're very proud to offer.

So, this is not just about money, it's for the client and for compensation for their injuries and their loss of quality of life, and to get them the medical treatment they need to get better physically and emotionally and compensated monetarily for them and for us. Our star is hitched to their star.

# What Types Of Personal Injury Cases Do You Handle?

Our primary focus is on motor vehicle accidents and injuries, including automobile accidents, motorcycle accidents, truck and 18-wheeler accidents, even ATV accidents and jet ski accidents; accidents involving any type of motorized or mechanical apparatus in which people can be injured due to someone else's negligence or wrongdoing. We also handle slip and fall cases, as well as product defect and product liability cases, in which a product does not perform as advertised and causes personal injury, such as a table saw that was defectively designed or manufactured and goes off-track, cutting off a hand, or a postage meter that falls apart and cripples someone due to faulty construction or design, or even beauty products that that cause allergic reactions or burns.

Additionally, we also handle dog bite cases. We are handling a case now in which a very large Doberman

Pinscher bit hard into a child's scalp and head, causing permanernt injuries and scarring. Another type of Personal Injury matter that we handle is Products liability cases. There are all kinds of situations, products, people and things that injure people due to someone else's negligence, including in the design or manufacture of a product.

## Is There A Particular Time Of Day That Auto Accidents Occur?

Looking back on the thousands of auto accident cases we've handled most automobile accidents occur during rush hour times, although many happen in the late evenings or early mornings, around midnight, and many of those have to do with some sort of substance abuse on the part of the person that injures our client. Those generally happen on Friday and Saturday nights around midnight till the early morning.

# Are Dog Bite Cases A Common Occurrence?

Dog bite cases are more common than most people think, but they also include a lot more than just bites; sometimes dogs chase someone and they pose a danger, even if they don't actually bite someone. The theme of dog bite cases is really this: they're like bad children, in that it's really not their fault, it's the dog's owner who's at fault.

They're at fault because they have allowed their dog to run loose or to get out of the house, garage or backyard without taking the proper precautions, such as an invisible fence, which is equipped with electronic sensors that give the dog a mild shock if they try to leave the premises. These are very effective but many dog owners won't take the time, effort and expense to install something like an invisible fence or even an actual fence; they just allow their dog run outside for a few minutes and use the neighborhood as a bathroom while they stand in the doorway in their robe because they don't want to go walk the dog.

That means their dog is now loose and very happy, which makes it a danger; even when it's trying to be friendly, accidents occur, which means a dog's natural instinct to play and chase

after moving objects puts people at risk, including joggers, children playing outside and people on bicycles and tricycles. All of these are potential victims of loose dogs, all because bad owners have chosen to not keep their dogs confined in a safe manner. That is the cause of most dog bites, and children are often the victims of dog bites because they're small and moving; the perfect target for large dogs.

Sometimes, the dog is just being playful, but when dog is bigger than a child, something bad can happen, and when they chase a bicycle or a jogger, something bad can happen, whether they are scratched or bitten or attempt to get away by running into the street and perhaps being hit by a car or falling over. Some dogs are a danger because the owner has permitted it; it's usually unintentionally but it's often out of selfishness.

There is a saying in Virginia that every dog is entitled to a free bite, which means that a dog's proclivity is to bite, because it is an animal. Therefore, when most dogs bite someone the first time, the burden is on the plaintiff and their attorney to prove the owner negligent in their maintenance of the dog. If an owner knows the dog has a proclivity to bite because it's bitten before, they'll be held liable most of the time, but if it's the first time, it's almost impossible to hold the owner liable for damages because every dog is entitled to one free bite.

# How Are Burn Injuries Typically Caused?

We see a lot of burn injuries! Most people think burns are the result of a fire, and most of the time they are, but there are many ways to get burned. We've had a number of clients who have been

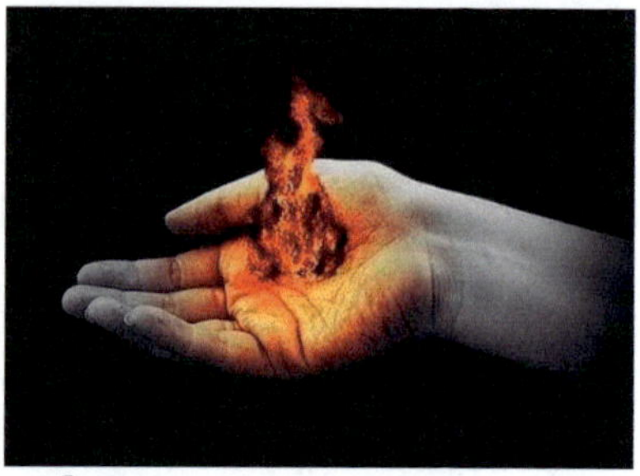

burned by defective products, such as a stove or a propylene gas cylinder, from different types of products that are used for welding and products with a high burn level, like a torch.

One of the more common ways that burn injuries occur is through the application of beauty products, such as facial and hair products, on the skin or the scalp,  when the product is defective or it has not been manufactured properly; perhaps they used some type of chemical and either failed to disclose it on the package or failed to give proper instructions with regard to the amount to be applied or how long something should be applied for coloring hair or having a facial or putting on some type of lotion.

Many people, particularly women, experience significant burns from beauty products, as well as loss of their hair, burned scalps and burned faces that leave behind scarring and disfigurement. It's not just about a fire in a house; burns can be caused by something a little more esoteric than the classic burning house.

# What Sort Of Trucking Accidents Have You Seen?

Statistically, personal injury lawyers don't see a significant number of trucking accidents, but when they do, they're usually significant cases simply by their nature; the size and weight of a large truck versus a car or motorcycle makes the damage caused by such accidents devastating. Whenever there is a trucking accident in which the trucker is at fault and operating the truck for their employer, because of the master/servant relationship, which is a doctrine of shared and shifted liability, the employer will almost always be considered liable for the acts of their trucker.

The way claims come about is to name the trucker and state whatever they may have done, such as running a red light or frequently driving for too many hours, if they're long-haul truckers. Most states have a period of time that a trucker can drive before they have to stop and get a certain amount of hours for sleep and rest, and in Virginia, the time limit is 12 hours. Many trucking accidents happen because drivers are tired, so they drift off and their truck goes out of control.

Because truckers are professional drivers, there are not a lot of trucking accidents, but when they do occur, they are usually quite devastating, whether they hit another vehicle from behind, or while in an intersection or when changing lanes on the Interstate when a vehicle is driving in their blind spot. The injuries and damages are usually significant, but you have to establish that it was a trucker's fault and not that of the other driver's but when it is established that the driver was negligent in their operation of the vehicle, they are held to a higher standard because they are professionals and they have to take extra care with regard to the operation of their truck, which is really a dangerous instrument.

There aren't many trucking accidents, but of those that occur, they're usually the fault of the trucker in some way, in exceeding the hours that they drive, the way that they drive, the chances they take and the speeds they go and the effect is usually devastating.

# How Soon After An Injury Should I Contact An Attorney?

Yesterday is probably the best answer, in order to get an idea of what needs to be done.

When people ask when they should get treatment for their injuries, I also give the same reply, because it puts them in the frame of mind that they need to immediately get help, which is the right frame of mind for a number of reasons.

Obviously, if they have been injured, they shouldn't wait to be treated, or to get the tests necessary to find out if there are internal injuries, fractured bones, herniated discs, or concussions or brain injuries. Tests like MRI and CAT scans, X-rays or blood tests may be necessary immediately in order to rule major injuries in or out. If the injuries are not major, the individual needs to follow up with medical care and physical therapy, chiropractic care or continued monitoring. These things are important to get under control, as is getting to the right healthcare providers as quickly as possible.

Another reason to get medical treatment immediately is for their personal injury claim because the longer a person waits to get medical treatment, the lower the value of their claim goes. The insurance company will assert that, if you're really hurt badly, you're going to get medical treatment immediately and, if not, you can't be hurt that badly. Delaying medical treatment can not only hurt you, it can also hurt your personal injury claim, since it'll appear that you weren't hurt that badly.

Another issue with medical treatment is gaps in treatment. Doctors and other healthcare providers will note in the person's medical history that they need additional follow-up or treatment, and those medical notes are necessary for a lawyer to review and evaluate the degree of their client's injury and present that to the insurance company, which will decide if they think the medical records show the reason, necessity and relation to the accident to see if they should be liable for treatment. These medical notes always say at the end if the person needs to come back in 6 weeks or one month or two weeks unless they're being discharged.

If an individual who is seeking medical treatment and has a personal injury claim does not follow the doctor's orders and they don't come back in two weeks, or they skip doctor, chiropractor or physical therapy appointments several times through the course of their treatment, insurance company adjusters will pick up on that immediately and suggest they're not badly injured, if they're missing so many appointments or they're not doing what their healthcare providers have told them to do, so they can't have that much pain and suffering, and therefore they should not be given so much money.

# The Benefits Of Retaining An Attorney For A Personal Injury Case

In Virginia, the levels of compensation for the negligence of another person's act that cause injury, such as the at-fault driver in a car accident who rear-ended someone as they stopped at a red light, will depend on establishing liability. Liability is necessary in a personal injury matter as a predicate to getting compensation, but once it's established, a personal injury attorney can get what are called compensatory damages. In Virginia, such damages fall into two categories; Special Damages and General Damages.

**Special Damages**

Special damages, or "Specials," are compensation for out-of-pocket expenses incurred, including the costs of all medical treatment if the person is found 100 percent. That means, if the medical bills are $50,000, then the other party's insurance company, the "Tortfeasor," will pay the full $50,000, or all of the medical bills incurred that are related to the accident, as well as the cost of prescriptions, the cost of taxis to get to doctor's appointments when the car is damaged or being repaired, subway receipts and anything else related to having to get to your doctor's or physical therapy appointment; this is all special damages.

Other expenses that the tortfeasor's insurance carrier may have to cover can also include hiring a gardener or a housekeeper because you're unable to do those things due to your injury. Of course, special damages also includes lost wages and income, including compensation for time you missed from work due to pain and suffering, inconvenience and doctor and therapy visits at your hourly, weekly or annualized rate of pay.

**General Damages**

General damages are what we call the area of pain, suffering, inconvenience, discomfort, scarring, disfigurement and permanent injuries in which someone loses a limb or sight or is paralyzed or permanently loses some degree of mobility. All of those items are compensable and therefore have to be assessed some type of monetary value if appropriate. An insurance company, judge or jury will ultimately determine the value of pain and suffering, inconvenience, discomfort and if applicable, scarring, disfigurement and permanent injury or permanent partial injury.

The art of being a personal injury lawyer is to determine a value of general damages and to convince an insurance adjuster that the degree of pain and suffering and all general damages is worth

that value. That is the real heart of a personal injury claim; medical bills are medical bills and prescription receipts are prescription receipts and lost wages are lost wages; all of those are easily verifiable and determinable. Establishing a value for general damages such as pain and suffering is the art of the personal injury lawyer.

# Common Mistakes People Make Upon Becoming Injured

One common mistake people make is to delay getting medical treatment, in part because many people are injured and don't realize it right after the accident. Perhaps they're upset by the accident and their adrenaline and endorphins are pumping through their system, and those

substances, which we produce when are in a flight or a fight state, can mask pain temporarily. Sometimes, an injury is not readily apparent because it's not a cut, bump or bruise; often, muscles, ligaments and tendons that are stretched and damaged in a car accident, in a slip and fall accident, in just about any accident, but they don't show up immediately.

Those types of injuries are not apparent right away because, although the muscles, ligaments and tendons have been stretched beyond the normal movement, many of the capillaries in the circulatory system are engorged with blood to heal the damage, and it's not until the person relaxes, perhaps when they go to sleep that night or the next that they begin to feel pain and knots and trigger points in their neck or their back or their legs.

That's why one of the most common mistakes is in not getting medical care immediately after an accident, even if they're not hurting at that moment, just to be on the safe side. When they do start to have symptoms, perhaps within a day or two or three of an accident, they delay and think it's not serious and they'll get over it in a day or so, and before they know it, it's been a week or more since the accident when they finally decide to get medical treatment. That will ultimately hurt them physically, but it will also hurt their claim, because the insurance company will claim they were not badly injured.

Another mistake people make after being injured in an accident is to not think about the impact of the injuries on themselves, their life and perhaps their families. They may end up being unable to provide for themselves or their family due to lost work, or they may not take care of themselves medically as they should and they may end up with some type of permanent injury that makes them old before their time.

Failing to speak to a personal injury lawyer immediately after an accident is a big mistake because the lawyer can steer their client to the right doctors and therapists as quickly as possible and they can monitor their treatment and suggest ways their client can maximize both their medical treatment and their compensation by being a good patient, which can turn into greater compensation.

Delay in getting medical treatment and delay in seeing a personal injury lawyer are the two biggest mistakes injured people make, but another is to apologize to the other party after an accident because they think they're being courteous. People talk too much after an accident too often, whether it's speaking to the other driver after an auto accident or to the store manager after a slip and fall. People get embarrassed when they're in accidents even if it's not their fault and, too often, anything they say will be taken out of context and used against them and make them look as if they do not have a claim.

# What Documents Are Necessary In A Personal Injury Claim?

Which documents are necessary will depend on the nature of the accident; for a motor vehicle accident that is someone else's fault, the potential client needs a copy of the police report. In Virginia, when police respond to a motor vehicle accident, they must make a full report of the accident, including information about the drivers, their history, a diagram of how the accident occurred and who's at fault.

The police report is done mainly for statistical purposes but it is available several days after the accident and it is very important to obtain, as is the information gathered in the exchange between drivers when the police respond, including names and addresses, driver's license and insurance information. If they have the names and contact information for any witnesses to the accident, those are absolutely critical to bring, as is a copy of their own automobile policy, since, unbeknownst to most people in Virginia, not only do they have liability coverage, but if an accident is their fault, they usually have something called medical payments coverage or medical expense coverage.

This is a form of no fault health insurance that says if you're in an accident and hurt by a car anywhere in the world, even if it's not your own car, you can submit the medical bills from that accident to your own insurance company and they will pay all of the medical bills directly to the insured, tax-free, up to whatever the MedPay or MedExpense policy limit, which is usually $5,000 or $10,000.

This is a windfall for the client; they don't know they have it 99 percent of the time, so I can look like a hero when I can show them an extra $5,000 or $10,000 in tax-free money. The best part is, they can still get all of their medical bills paid a second time by the tortfeasor's insurance company.

That's a double windfall, but it can get better; if their health insurance pays most of their medical bills, they can see a triple recovery by law in Virginia ethically, morally and legally; they can collect the total value of all of the medical bills as special

damages from the at-fault party's insurance company, get the payment of their medical bills up to the policy limits on their own medical payments coverage and their health insurance company will also most of their medical expenses. At the same time, the plaintiff's and defendant's insurance companies get no credits or offsets for any of those payments.

If the case is a slip and fall accident, the client will want to bring a store incident report, usually filled out by a manager, as well as names and contact information for any witnesses to your slip and fall, and the names of the wrongdoer or the company that caused the injury. For a product liability case, you'll need the name of the company who sold the product and the manufacturer of the product that hurt you, the labels and containers from the product, and receipts for the product. All of this information should be provided to an attorney immediately for them to investigate and establish liability and begin organizing a plan of action to get the maximum possible compensation for their client.

# How Do Insurance Companies Operate In An Auto Accident Case?

With auto accidents, several things begin to occur almost immediately after the accident that can make a victim's head spin; first, the at-fault party's insurance company will, within days of the accident or even sooner, begin to call the injured party and ask for recorded statement from them on the phone about what happened.

The worst thing they can do is to give a recorded statement to the other person's insurance company until they talk to and retain an attorney, who may or may not allow them to give a recorded statement, although they'll usually advise against it, until after they've organized aspects of the claim and coached the client, and even then, only with the attorney present.

When the other party's insurance company contacts them for a recorded statement, they'll ask questions in a way that attempts to minimize the responsibility of their insured and try to open up another front against the accident victim, to make them seem at fault and therefore cancel out any type of recovery. They will ask questions that seem innocuous, such as, “Good morning, how are you?” hoping that you’ll answer like everyone else and say, “I’m fine, how are you?” That’s on a recorded statement, however, so later

on in the claims process, they have the victim a day or two after the accident saying, “I’m fine.” The pitfalls of giving a recorded statement to an insurance company are numerous and unfathomably deep, so don’t do it.

The second issue is that of your own insurance company in an auto accident, because you have an obligation to call them anytime you’re in an accident, whether it’s your fault or not, because you have a contract, and they need to know about the history of everything related to your car. More importantly, if the other driver does not have insurance or they’re underinsured, you’ll need them to cover the claim. Everyone in the state of Virginia carries uninsured motorist coverage just in case, but if you don’t report the accident in a timely fashion to your company; you can lose the right to uninsured motorist coverage, so contact them immediately.

In terms of moving forward from the accident, liability has to be established, so the insurance company will look at the police crash report, talk to the police officer and talk to their insured, talk to any witnesses and from all of that, will determine if they're going to accept the liability and pay a claim on behalf of the party who is not at fault. That process can take the insurance company several weeks or months, but after that, it's a matter of the personal injury attorney, on behalf of their client, staying in touch with the other insurance company, giving them periodic reports about their client, including their treatment status and their injuries.

Once their client has finished treatment related to the accident, the attorney will get all of the medical bills, medical reports, prescription receipts; everything out-of-pocket expense incurred that's related to the accident, and submit a claim to the other party's insurance company. They will then negotiate with that insurance company and try to get a settlement the client and the insurance company are satisfied with. Most cases settle out of court, although some go to trial.

# What Is The Statute Of Limitations For Personal Injury Cases?

The basic statute of limitations in Virginia is two years, which means a person must either file a lawsuit or settle their claim against the wrongdoer's insurance company within two years of the date of the accident. That seems very clear, but it's not; if my client had an accident on January 1st 2015, that doesn't mean you have to file your lawsuit or settle the case by no later than January 1st 2017, it means you have until December 31, 2016, so if you thoughtlessly file it on January 1st, you'd be out of luck because you would not have filed your lawsuit or settled your claim in a timely fashion, by missing the two-year cut off by one day.

Your lawsuit must be filed or your claim settled within two years of the date of the accident, not on the second anniversary; unfortunately many people make that mistake. The statute of limitations exists to give accident victims time to get well or to find out they won't. If the second anniversary of the accident is approaching, the attorney has to file a lawsuit to stop the statute of limitations from running. At that point, they have one year to try to get the patient well or settle the lawsuit, but near the end of that year, if the client is still not well and being treated, you can file what's called a "non-suit," which temporarily dismisses the suit for 6 months, after which the suit can be re-filed and get another year.

In reality, while the statute of limitations is two years, through good lawyering and utilizing different aspects of Virginia law, it's possible to extend the time to settle the case or go to trial by about four or more years, so that your client is well and is in shape to go a trial or try and settle it if you have to buy more than two years.

For children, the statute of limitations is two years after their 18th birthday, unless they become emancipated early, or their parents can file on their behalf. If the court allows them to be emancipated at 16, then they only have two years from that to have their case settled or to file a lawsuit filed. However, while children have quite a long time to file, the parents have 5 years from the date of the accident to file a lawsuit or settle their claim for the medical bills they have incurred on behalf of their child.

If a child is injured, there is a bifurcated statute of limitations; the child has two years after they turn 18 to file a lawsuit, have it filed for them or to settle, while the parent has five years. Also, the parents can only recover for child's medical bills; the child has a separate claim for pain and suffering and inconvenience and discomfort.

# How Long Can A Personal Injury Case Potentially Last?

Every personal injury case has its own rhythm and time-frame, so each case will take as long as it needs to take for the client to get all of the treatment they need from their healthcare providers

and to reach maximum medical improvement from the accident. The accident obviously caused deficits in their life; pain and the inability to do certain physical things they could do before, perhaps missing work or not being able to go bowling or to do chores; they may have to learn to live with and manage pain.

These types of damages are incurred in an accident and. Eventually, the person gets to the point where their healthcare providers will clear them and say there is nothing more that medical science can do for you; the orthopedic doctor has done their thing, the neurologist has done their thing and the physical therapist likewise; all tests are all done and you are released from medical care. It is then that personal injury attorneys shift into high gear and begin the claim process; obtaining all medical records, bills and receipts for out-of-pocket expenses, test results and all lost wage documentation for their client and put it all together.

Then, the attorney will review everything, so as to understand what happened to them, in order to be able to express the degree of pain and suffering, inconvenience and discomfort, loss of quality of life, possible scarring and disfigurement to the insurance company, as well as to develop a value for all of it. While it's true that it's impossible to put a value on pain and loss of quality of life. That's why the attorney earns their 33 1/3 percent contingency fee that is taken from the lump sum settlement that includes medical bills and lost wages and pain and suffering.

All of that information is submitted to the insurance company and the case is negotiated; probably 98-99% of cases are settled out of court through negotiations between the client's attorney, the insurance company adjuster and the opposing parties, all of whom are looking to reach a settlement amount the client is happy with. If the client is not happy with the final amount the insurance company is willing to pay, the client has to choose between taking it or filing a lawsuit, which only happens about two percent of the time because everyone has an incentive to settle a claim out of court, given that trials can be long and costly for everyone.

In Virginia, a person in an accident case has two years from the date of the accident to either settle their case or file a lawsuit. The filing of a lawsuit stops the statute of limitations and sets another series of smaller statutes of limitations in motion; the client has another year to try and settle the case with the insurance company if the client is still treating and didn't get well within two years.

You file the lawsuit to preserve the client's rights, not to serve the defendant, the person who injured your client; the attorney will just file the lawsuit, without being actively involved in fighting it at that point; they are just buying another year for them to get well. Hopefully, they get well within that third year and, if they do, the case may be able to settle.

If the client gets better, then most of the time you'll settle it before that year is up, but if they're still not well by the end of that third year, it's necessary to decide whether you want to serve the defendant, which means having the lawsuit papers given to a sheriff or a private process server to track down the defendants and hand them a copy, which is called service of process, or you can take what's called a voluntarily nonsuit.

A voluntary nonsuit is something available in Virginia, in which you file a document asking the court to temporarily dismiss your lawsuit. It is entered by a judge of the Circuit Court, and says that your case is being dismissed without prejudice but that you'll be re-filing it again within six months of the date nonsuit order is signed by the judge. This buys you another six months for the client to perhaps get better and try and settle the case.

If you can't settle it and your client is still not well by the end of six months, you re-file your lawsuit; you just take another clean copy to the clerk of the court and have it stamped and filed before the six months is up. If you do that, it's back on the court's radar and you have another year to either settle the case or serve the defendant with the lawsuit.

If you don't settle it within the year or serve the defendant, you lose all rights and you're barred forever from any recovery. However, you're moving into the second part of your third year, so you bought yourself up to four-and-a-half years from the date of the accident for the client to get well or negotiations to continue. There are no other options, there are no more nonsuits you can take, no more of the tricks of the trade to delay it for your client's benefit. You now must either settle it at the end of this four-and-a-half-year period or serve the defendant.

Once you serve the defendant, then you are off and running, and there are time periods for you to do things and for the other party to do things under the Rules of Circuit Court. There is no set period of time for the lawsuit from the time the defendant is served to trial, but it can take as long as 18 months, depending on the complexity of the injuries to your client and the complexities of the issues and liability of the case.

Between interrogatories filed by both sides, request for production of documents filed by both sides during what is called discovery, doing requests for admissions, having your client undergo an independent mental exam by the insurance doctors to determine if all the injuries are reasonable and necessarily related to the accident; all of that takes time. Then comes scheduling and sitting down for depositions; the insurance company will take the deposition of your client, to talk about the accident, their injuries and their medical history and you will take the deposition of the driver of the car to establish that they were at fault.

These things can take up to a year and a half before you have a trial. There have been cases in which accident cases took more than five years before a final judgment is rendered for a client, although that is very unusual. Most – about 95 percent – of the thousands of personal injury cases I have handled over nearly 30 years have settled with my clients being satisfied and happy and the money they received was tax-free and came within the two-year original statute of limitations.

# The First Steps To Take After Sustaining An Injury

The first step immediately following any accident, whether it's an automobile accident, a slip, trip and fall accident or a products liability accident, in which you were injured by a product that you own hurts you, is to make sure you are okay. Take an inventory of yourself immediately to determine where you are hurt and how bad it seems.

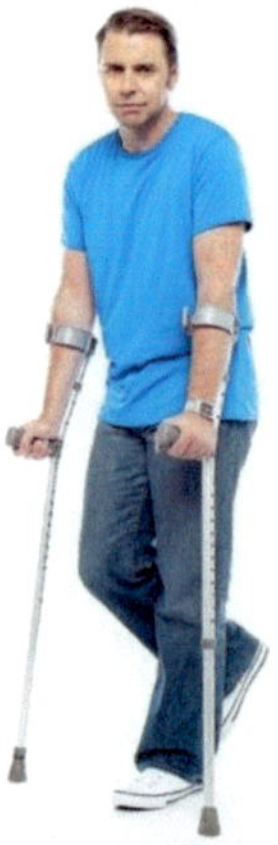

When people are in accidents, an autonomic part of their system, called the flight or fight mechanism, takes over and unconsciously and puts the body on high alert and begins to pump endorphins, steroids and adrenaline into their body and brain, and they gain extra strength and even mask or cover up much of the pain they may normally have.

Often, you don't know how badly you are hurt when you are in an accident because your body and brain are producing all of these hormones and chemicals to mask much of the potential pain and suffering. Therefore, you should begin to take stock of your body immediately after the accident; if an ambulance arrives and the EMTs recommend that you get medical treatment, don't be brave about it, just go to the hospital and let the professionals decide if there is anything wrong with you, seriously or otherwise.

Also, while you're feeling less pain because of the hormones and chemicals racing through your body, get all the information you can from the person who injured you, including their driver's license information, the car's license plate numbers and the make

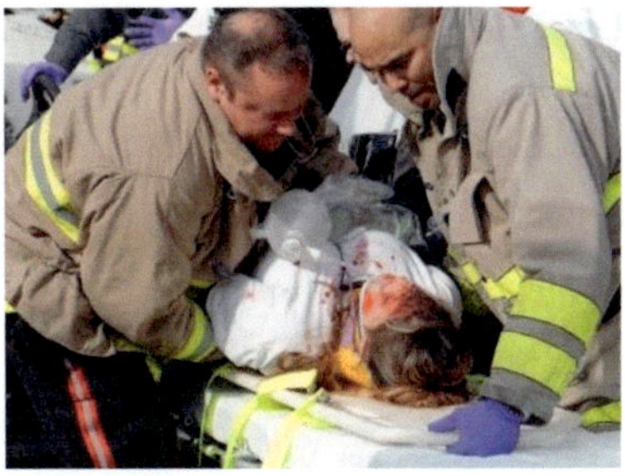

and model of their car, and all of their insurance information. Use your smartphone to take pictures of the damage to both cars, a picture of the other driver and, if you're hurt in any way, pictures of any visible injuries. Someone will also have to call the police to look at the accident and write up a police crash report.

The police may be able to help you with an exchange of information between you and the other driver, if necessary, because such information is important and needs to be obtained at the accident scene. An analysis of how badly you feel and whether you need to go to the hospital in an ambulance, photographs, videos, information about the other driver and their insurance company, the call to the police and the officer's report; collect anything that seems relevant, because it's all important.

After that, you will probably need medical care; we're talking about a personal injury case and it may be that you wake up the next day feeling like a truck ran over you because the muscles and ligaments and tendons of your body are pulled and torn, even though that was not apparent at the time of the accident. Then, you're off to the emergency room or to your primary doctor for treatment, then to orthopedists and physical therapists; that is the genesis of a personal injury claim, because the most important thing being taking care of your health. Money is secondary to health, but after you've done all of the above, you'll then need to contact an experienced personal injury attorney that has handled thousands of personal injury cases over 20-plus years. This should be your criteria for retaining the services of a personal injury attorney. Giving them one-third of the lump sum of the settlement, as we previously discussed, is cheap at twice the price because you don't pay for anything upfront; it only comes out of the insurance company settlement later.

# What Are Some Qualities To Consider When Looking For Personal Injury Attorneys?

The first thing to look for in a personal injury attorney is to make sure they have a great deal of experience in handling personal injury cases because there is no substitute for experience.

You don't want somebody learning on your case, you'd rather have someone who has handled at least 1,000 personal injury cases in their career and to be at the top of their profession, after practicing law for 20 years or more. That would be my criteria if I were to hire a personal injury attorney.

Where can you find a personal injury attorney? There are many resources; online resources and referrals from friends or relatives are always good sources. If you're checking online, using AVVO.com is probably the best place to start; your criteria should be to find an attorney who has a rating of 9 out of 10 stars, which means they are the top of their profession in terms of industry recognition, experience, success and lack of any major discipline issues. Everything you are looking for in an attorney can be searched at AVVO.com, and it will show their years in practice, any publications and so on and with a rating of 9 or above, you can be assured that they are the kind of attorney you might want to handle your case. Those are the exterior criteria.

The interior criteria would be your comfortability with the attorney, so you want to interview at least two or three personal injury attorneys who meet the exterior criteria I talked about; talk to them on the phone, listen to their tone of voice, how they address and talk with you, how they answer your questions, meaning whether they answer truthfully, honestly and straightforwardly or deceptively and evasively and in generalities; obviously, you want the former, not the latter. Find out if they seem to be able to answer your questions crisply and precisely, and do they have a warm and engaging personality and presence and, perhaps, a little bit of a sense of humor also. If they have those qualities on the phone, they will have those qualities in person and you should meet them in person, so that you and the attorney can size each other up and decide

whether or not you have a legitimate good claim to pursue.

An attorney doesn't want to take a case in which they will spend a lot of time and their own money pursuing, since you're paying nothing upfront, and then end up with nothing for you; they don't want to hurt their client and their expectations or yourself, so they'll get that cleared away in the beginning as to whether or not you have a legitimate, good, winning personal injury case. If they do that, then you'll probably have a winning team, with you and the attorney working together on your case.

# How Is Someone Compensated If The Other Party Has No Insurance?

Fortunately, it does not happen often, but it does happen. The reason why it does not happen often is because most states, including Virginia, require drivers to carry uninsured motorist

coverage, in addition to both bodily injury and property damage liability insurance. That means, if you're in an accident and it's your fault, your insurance company will pay the victim's personal injuries and property damages up to a certain limit, and also, uninsured motorist coverage, which will pay the bills even if the at-fault driver isn't following the law.

In 95 percent of the cases I have handled over nearly 30 years, when my clients have been injured by another motorist, their liability insurance covered my client and paid their medical bills, lost wages and pain and suffering for the personal injury claim. In the other five percent, the person who injures my client may not have insurance; perhaps they are simply too poor to afford it, or they lost their insurance or it lapsed, and they shouldn't be driving, but in those cases, the uninsured motorist coverage kicked in.

Uninsured motorist coverage means you are paying for liability coverage for yourself when the other driver does not have insurance. When that kicks in, your insurance company actually becomes the other driver's insurance company and stands behind them and will cover your personal injury claim as if they had insurance, up to the policy limits of your uninsured motorist coverage. That is to protect each of us from the irresponsibility of people who drive without insurance.

That is how you're compensated when the other person has no liability insurance coverage on their motor vehicle. As a result, in about 99.9% of automobile cases, there is coverage for personal injuries incurred and personal injury claims, from either the other person's liability policy or from your own uninsured motorist coverage taking care of you when the other person doesn't have insurance.

## How Is One Compensated If They Are Unable To Work After An Accident?

In Virginia, a personal injury claim has three basic parts that make up the whole of a lump sum settlement and those parts are; compensation from the other person's insurance company for the totality of all medical bills incurred, the lost wages incurred and for your pain and suffering, inconvenience and discomfort. Those are the three slices that make up the whole pie. In the part that deals with lost wages, an individual who is injured is entitled to have their lost wages paid for the amount of time that they missed from work at their hourly or annual rate of pay for all of the days and hours they missed from work due to pain and suffering, doctor's visits, therapy visits and any other lost time related to their injury.

Most of the time, that is self-limiting because, by the time the two-year statute of limitations runs out, 95 percent of accident victims have finished treating, they are back to where they were before the accident started and they no longer have a need for medical treatment, they are no longer losing time from work and the claim is either moving toward settlement or has already been settled. However, there are a few cases in which a person is injured so badly that they not only lose wages from the time of the accident to the time a lawsuit must be filed that a doctor will say the person is permanently, partially disabled, possibly to the extent that they will never be able to do their job again.

That depends upon the doctor's evaluation of their injuries and how they would affect them doing their job. The doctor must get to know them, understand what type of work they do; whether it is manual labor, or they are sedentary all day, running around and driving all day for their job, it all factors into the evaluation of whether that person can work part time or do light duty in the future or perhaps even have to take a new job because of their injuries.

When this happens, a person is entitled to future lost wages and loss of earning capacity and it is an art to calculate all of this; it's like you are looking into a crystal ball into the future trying to determine how long a person will likely live, based on actuarial statistics having to do with their age and health at the time of the accident, how long they would have normally lived and how long they would normally work.

People usually retire before they die and actuarial tables are used to calculate their life and the normal length of their career, along with the nature of their job. They probably have a work history, and there are calculations that can figure out what that person would have made over the next 20 or 30 or 40 years of their work life, building in reasonable expectations for inflation and raises and promotions that would likely have occurred based on their past performance and the nature of their business and injury and their job.

These computer models can predict what the person likely would have made going forward into the future, and we can figure out how much compensation they are entitled to for their inability to work anymore. If it can be defined this way, they are entitled to recover for their loss of earning capacity and future lost wages by using the criteria available at present. By the way, those lost wages are reduced to the present day value of what they would be and can often be given in a lump sum as part of the settlement calculus or they can be part of a structured settlement going forward, in which the person receives so much per month or a year, like an annuity, based upon the calculations of what they may have made had they not been in the accident.

## HOW DOES AN ATTORNEY GET PAID FOR A PERSONAL INJURY CASE?

A personal injury attorney is different from other type of attorneys, such as tax, criminal, maritime and estates and trusts attorneys, who get paid either a flat fee or on an hourly basis,

because we are compensated on a contingency fee basis, which means that the attorney takes the risk that there may be no money at the end of the case, no pot of gold at the end of the rainbow.

When the person finishes treating and going forward, there may be questions of liability or questions of insurance coverage and money available to cover the client's damages and injuries; there is a risk in accepting a personal injury case because a small minority of cases won't pan out for one reason or another. Perhaps there is no actual insurance coverage available or there are issues of liability because, in Virginia, if a client is even one percent at fault and the other party is 99 percent at fault, it's called contributory negligence and your client cannot recover anything. Issues of liability are not always clear in the beginning.

A personal injury attorney doesn't have a contract for hourly billing or a flat fee; they get nothing upfront; they typically get paid one-third of the final lump-sum settlement amount. Since they are paid on a contingency fee basis, they take a risk that there is a small chance they will get nothing, which does very occasionally happen. Therefore, they are allowed to charge something like one-third (or 40 percent if the case goes to trial) of the total amount of the amount a client receives, either through settlement negotiations or through a judge or jury after a trial.

The attorney gets one-third of that total lump sum, which is made up of three things; the total lost wages, loss of future earning capacity and all of the medical bills and other costs incurred, as well as money for pain and suffering and continuous discomfort and scarring disfigurement, if appropriate. The lawyer takes one-third off the top of that before any or all bills are paid and before any liens are settled; the attorney has a priority lien of that one-third against settlement.

For example, if the lump sum settlement is $90,000, the attorney gets $30,000 and the client gets $60,000 tax free. It's tax free for the client, not the attorney. In return, they work for days, weeks, months or years with absolutely no money or fees upfront. The clients always remain responsible for the expenses incurred in a personal injury matter, such as the lawyer paying in advance to get copies of medical records and bills, police crash reports; items like that, although those costs are usually nominal.

# What Should I Do If The Insurance Company Contacts Me After An Accident?

There are usually two insurance companies involved in an auto accident case; yours and the opposing party's, and since you were injured and they are the bad guys, their insurance company wants to pay you as little as possible. The other

insurance company is the client's; the one for the person who has been injured, your client's insurance company. People often forget about their own insurance company when they are in an accident that is and it is someone else's fault because they know the other person's insurance company has to pay them, but let's start with their own.

The injured client has an absolute duty to notify their own insurance company as soon as possible when they are in an accident; that's part of every insurance contract. One reason to do that anyway is because, what if the person who injured you doesn't have insurance or it lapsed and they don't even know? You want to notify your own insurance company about the accident to protect your interests or to be able to pursue an uninsured motorist claim should it become necessary, but if you don't notify them in a timely manner; they may refuse to fulfill your uninsured motorist coverage.

With your own insurance company, you want to be open and forthright with them about what occurred in the accident and be factually correct. However the other person's insurance company (we'll call it the bad guy's insurance company) is not your friend; they are, in essence, your enemy; their job is to protect the best interests of their insured, as well as the shareholders or owners, officers and directors of their company, which means they want to save them money and pay out as little as possible to you, the victim, in an insurance claim.

Assuming you are going to obtain the services of an attorney shortly after an accident, even though it could take several days or weeks to find the attorney you want, you should not speak to the other person's insurance company. You should never give a recorded statement to the other person's insurance company. Why?

Consider that most of the survey will be pleasant and proper and nice and casual and friendly; the insurance company will try to seem like a friend when they meet and greet us, asking you how you're doing, but what do we always say? We say we're doing fine. Unfortunately, that's being recorded, and months later, when you and your attorney are trying to settle your accident case, the adjuster will remind us that you told an adjuster you were fine right after the accident and that they have it on tape; then they'll ask why you're claiming you're badly hurt now, and claiming thousands of dollars in medical bills for previous year, when you said you were fine a day or two after?

That is why you don't want to speak to the other person's insurance company; let your attorney to do that. You only want to speak to the other person's insurance company with regard to the damage to your motor vehicle, and only to tell them where your car is so they can send their property damage adjuster to look at it and figure out whether it's totaled and give you the fair market value for it or, if it's damaged, what repairs should be done and where. Those things are okay to talk to the bad guy's insurance company about only in a very factual way; don't be led into conversations about how you feel or what happened in the accident with the other person's insurance company.

That's why God made personal injury lawyers; you contact them to speak to the bad guy's insurance company, not you. However, you certainly can and must cooperate with your own insurance company; in most cases, you do not need your attorney to do that.

# How Much Weight Do Photographs Carry In A Personal Injury Case?

There is an old Confucian or Chinese proverb that says, "A picture is worth a thousand words." Unfortunately, most attorneys are too wordy. We probably talk too much, when we probably should allow pictures, photographs, drawings, blueprints,

demonstrative evidence like that do our speaking for us because they speak louder and paint the picture of accidents and injuries and their aftermath more vibrantly. Photographs and pictures are extremely important; the sooner and the more, the better. Right after an accident, if you're able to, get out your smartphone and start taking pictures and videos of everything, including the damage to both vehicles, not just yours, something that many people forget to do.

They'll take pictures of the damage to their vehicle right after the accident, and not take any of the bad guy's car, because they only care about theirs, but in reality, when you are putting a personal injury claim together, you want to be able to vividly show an insurance adjuster or a judge or jury the dramatic impact that caused your personal injuries by showing them the damage to the car that hit you, as well as the damage to yours. That completes a great detailed picture of how strong the impact was that caused your personal injuries, plus the more property damage that was done to the two vehicles, the more likely the adjuster or the judge or jury, being human, will assume the personal injury was to you.

If it's a slip, trip and fall case, you want to take pictures, if possible, of where and what you fell on, whether it a loose railing on a stairway going down that caused you to fall, or you tripped on a rug that was not tacked down properly, or a hole that was left in a sidewalk, or water or other fluids or banana peels or grapes or ice cream or soft drinks that may have spilled on floors or stairways that caused you to slip and fall.

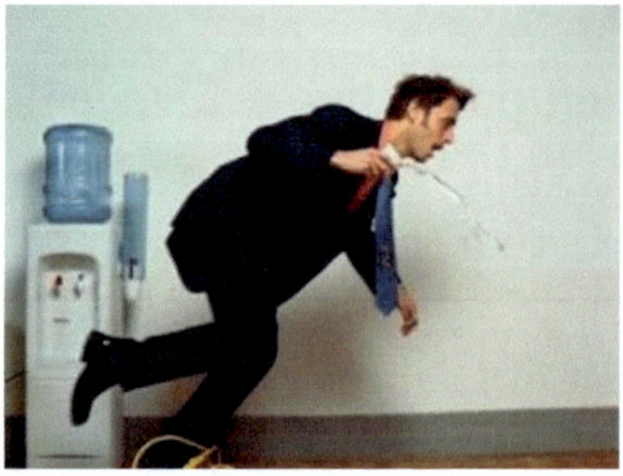

Likewise, if an electrical product blew up and injured you, taking pictures of the product that's left over and the pieces of it are all important. You want to take pictures of injuries that are visible as soon as possible, preferably at the scene of the accident or shortly thereafter and then take them in the doctor's office and continue to take them every day, maybe even several times a day. If you have cuts, burns, bruises or contusions, all of those things are highly important to give to the insurance adjuster or judge or jury to show the degree of your injury and then, to impute the degree of pain and suffering that must have occurred as a result of the dramatic pictures you take to show the stitches and resulting scars.

Scarring and disfigurement are extremely important and must be documented by photographing them constantly from the beginning. We come full circle to a picture is worth a thousand words; they can create the necessary total view of why you are complaining about the injuries, the pain and the suffering and disfigurement you are suffering from, which means we can put a monetary value on that for settlement or trial.

# What Is The Most Difficult Aspect Of A Personal Injury Case For An Attorney To Deal With?

The single most difficult thing we have to deal with is the insurance company; that's where the rubber meets the road; the only thing a personal injury attorney can do is to be direct about it and

get compensation from the insurance company for the client. That's the only job we really have in personal injury, to get compensation for the medical bills and lost wages incurred and, the most important, for the pain and suffering, the inconvenience and discomfort that they have suffered due to the negligence of another person.

The insurance company has the gold and the golden rule is often "He who has the gold makes the rules." As a graphic picture, we have an injured person who has hopefully gotten good medical care; we refer our clients to physicians for our clients that we know are very good and we are proud to do that. They will hold onto their bills until settlement, but the medical part is the single most important aspect for the client because, while money comes and goes, they only get one body.

Once they are done treating, I go in to action to get that person money for what they have suffered; the art of it is mainly getting the money for the pain and suffering part. The insurance company has the money, so initially we have to go hat in hand to them to ask for voluntary compensation, a voluntary settlement, on behalf of our client and they can call the shots. It's their money and, at that stage of settlement negotiations, they have the gold and they make the rules; they don't have to pay a penny voluntarily. They can be made to pay that penny by going to trial and having a judge or jury decide the value of the claim, but most insurance companies don't want to go to trial, which is good because most clients don't want to, either.

Everyone has to find a way to split the loaf of bread and the insurance company holds all the cards in the beginning; we have the threat of taking the insurance company and their insured to trial if they don't voluntarily give us something close to what we are asking for. The most difficult part is this stage of a personal injury claim is submitting a claim package, having the insurance company review it and then beginning negotiations. Most cases settle, which can be an agonizing and difficult process, but that's what we're paid for; that is the art of the deal, although it is the most challenging.

# THE ROLE OF SOCIAL MEDIA IN A PERSONAL INJURY CASE

Ninety-nine times out of a hundred, social media tends to hurt a person's personal injury case. By definition, social media is social and chatty; it's "What did you do today?" and "Here's what I did today" and "Here's how I am feeling", and "Here's the activities I am doing" and "Here's what I have done at work." Such chatter can potentially expose the client to actual problems with the insurance company, by giving them the ability to misinterpret what's going on in the client's life.

For instance, if they are told to stay in bed, but they post the picture of themselves out riding a bike, that is going against medical advice and may also indicate the person is not that badly injured. It's, "What is your day?" and "What have you been doing?"

More importantly, people are self-centered, so it's more, "Here's what I did today" and "Here's who I did it with" and those are activities that can potentially indicate the person is not that badly injured. Therefore, it is best to keep activity on social media to a minimum if you have a personal injury case; of course, even if you are not chatting and posting about yourself, other people, like friends, family or work colleagues may be asking you questions, or they may be putting posts on Facebook or Twitter and putting you in a position to have to answer and your answer may be misinterpreted. It's best to tell everybody, "Cool it! I'm not in the social media game now. I have a job to do, which is to take care of myself, to get well and then I'll be back in the game."

# What Factors Make A Personal Injury Case Difficult To Win?

There is rarely a perfect personal injury case scenario; every one of them has problems, deficits, holes and issues. The major issue is the question of liability, which means proving that the other person who caused your client's injury truly at fault,

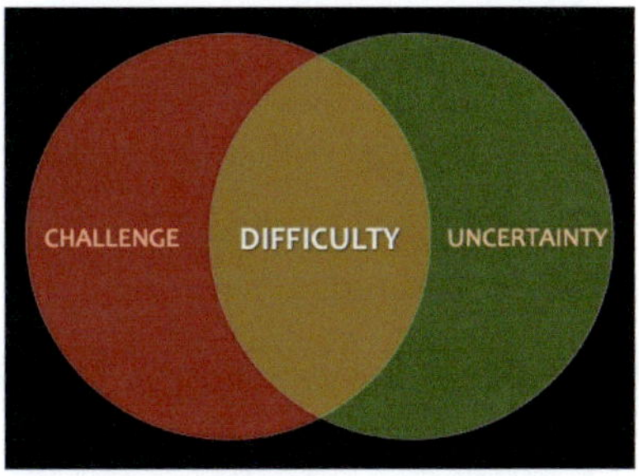


and were they negligent in doing or not doing something that caused injury to your client? The biggest issue can be the question of liability; that is the first threshold, wicket or door we have to go through to get to any possibility of compensation.

If the other person is not at fault or can't be shown to be at fault within a reasonable degree of certainty, there is no case. There may be injuries and treatments but there is no money and no case. Rarely are there perfect situations that indicate liability from the outset. About the only type of case that comes close to being a slam dunk from the liability side is a rear-end motor vehicle accident because there is never a good reason for one driver to strike another in the rear – none, zero.

The only exception to that would come if the person in front struck and injured the car in the rear, such as they were at a stoplight and the front car backed up for some reason. In a case like that, there may not be any liability on the part of the person in front, because it's considered reckless driving to back up on a highway in Virginia and a person doing something that is against traffic law is more likely to be found at least partly liable.

When you have two parties at fault and in Virginia, which is a contributory negligence state, if the injured party is even one percent at fault there is absolutely no personal injury case. That means no money, no recovery, no compensation to be had. That can be one of the biggest problems outside of a pure rear end car accident with your client stopped at a light or a stop sign, which is close to perfect a case as you can get for liability. Every other case can result in a struggle to convince an insurance adjuster or eventually a judge or jury that there was complete negligence on the other party's part and that your client is free of any negligence. That is probably one of the biggest issues in a personal injury case.

# CAN A GOOD ATTORNEY ESTIMATE MY CHANCES OF WINNING A PERSONAL INJURY CASE?

Yes, they would be able to because that is different from predicting how much they might recover. When you first talk to an attorney on the phone and have a consultation with them, then the number and types of questions they will ask will be significant with regard to the issue of how the accident occurred, including the when, where and how of the dynamics and mechanics of the accident because they are trying to establish whether or not it is worth their time and trouble and the time and trouble of the potential client to take on the case.

The attorney has to be convinced that there is at least a 51 percent chance or better that the case will settle or will be won at a jury or a judge trial. If it meets the threshold test, and it is more than 51 percent likelihood of there being compensation at the end of the rainbow after handling their case. After a couple hours of conversation, asking questions and taking notes and reviewing the documents, police reports, the attorney should be able to tell them with quite good certitude whether or not they have a good and legitimate personal injury case that is worth their time and trouble and the attorney's time and trouble to undertake and pursue.

# What Is An Example Of A Personal Injury Case Not Worth Pursuing?

The rules of the road state that if I got struck from the rear, it is totally the other person's fault, unless the person in the front vehicle is backing up, which means they won't recover anything because they are partially at fault. Another type or class of case that is risky, difficult and has to be entered into with great caution are slip, trip and fall cases. When someone slips and falls on some type of substance on the floor at a grocery store or a mall, or someone slips in a parking lot, or steps in a hole or trips on a sidewalk, these types of cases that are very difficult to establish liability; just because someone slips, trips and falls inside or outside a store or in some private area, is not in and of itself a definition of liability for the property owner or landlord or a business owner.

Just having an accident does not mean the store owner is at fault because they are not an absolute insurer of one's safety even if they invite them in to shop in their store. If a person falls in the store onto something on the floor, they can't be expected to clean the floors every minute and they can't post employees every five feet throughout the store to make sure someone doesn't fall, so if kids come in with ice cream or something falls off the shelf or a grape falls off the produce stand and someone slips and falls on these hazards doesn't mean the landlord will have to pay or is liable; the landlord must have reasonable notice and take reasonable precautions to address hazards on the floor.

Such cases are not an absolute, so slip and fall cases like this depend upon whether we can show there is actual notice that the property owner or the businessperson knew there was a hazard on the floor and hadn't cleaned it up, which is almost impossible to prove, or constructive notice, which means the hazard was present for an unreasonable period of time and the business owner should have seen it and taken care of it, but didn't. That is probably the riskiest type of personal injury case to take on.

# Can An Attorney Predict How The Case Will Proceed And How Much Compensation May Be Awarded?

The attorney can and should give the client an anatomy of a typical personal injury case that fits the facts as the client describes them and tests them for liability of the person that injured them, and come up with a

determination if the attorney believes there is a 51 percent chance or better that the person who injured them is liable and there will be compensation coming, based on their physical and mental state and injuries, what the medical course will be and how long it may take, although keep in mind, the attorney is not a doctor.

If they are experienced, they can give estimates of the types of likely doctors that will be seen during the course of treatment, the likely types of treatments or therapies that may be required and over what period of time it will take for the person to reach maximum medical improvement. Those are ranges based upon an attorney's experience, not about being a doctor. The attorney will advise them that once the person is done treating, they will get the medical records and bills from the healthcare providers, review everything, put a claim package together, send it to the insurance company, tell them that it's going to take a month or two for the lawyer to get all the records and bills.

It will then take the insurance company about a month to review everything and begin negotiations, which can take a day, a week, a month or even six months, depending on the good faith in negotiations, the degree of injuries and that type of thing. That's the anatomy of a personal injury case and things don't get resolved in days or weeks, but months and years. A good attorney can tell a client at that point how much they might be able to get at the end of the day.

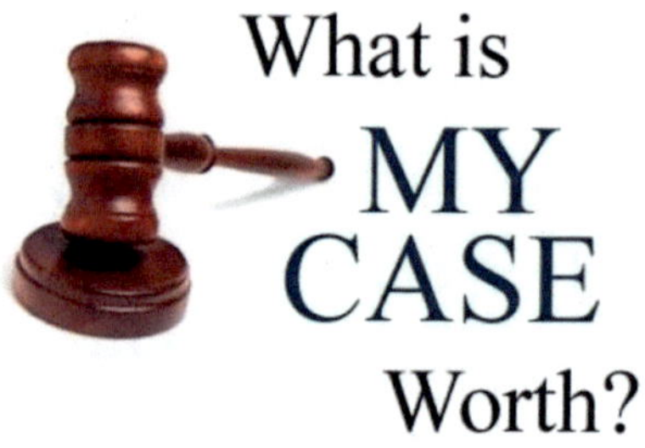


I absolutely refuse to do that at the beginning of the relationship, on the first day when they ask that ultimate question that everyone always asks on the first and last interview, all the way through to the middle of negotiations. I will never ever tell a client what I think they will get because there are so many variables, even up to the last minute. It's dangerous, it creates unfair expectations, which is not good for the client or the attorney.

## What Are The Most Common Types Of Personal Injury Cases?

The most common types of cases are motor vehicle accidents including motorcycle accidents, while the least common are probably dog bite and bicycle accident cases. The second-most common would be slip, trip and fall and third would be everything else, which is just a mixed bag.

## Do Clients Ever Get Discouraged From Pursuing A Personal Injury Case?

Yes. They get discouraged often with the pace of the medical treatment because it's often longer and more intense than they imagines at the beginning, maybe weeks and weeks of physical therapy and they have to take off work for half a day to go see a doctor or physical therapist. They are in pain, they tend to get touchy, their expectations can often be too high, they tend to be tired because they're usually not sleeping well because of their injuries.

The length of time it takes for a claim to be ripe and mature, or for even beginning negotiations after their treatment and then the pace of negotiations is just extremely frustrating to clients, even when you walk them through the process in the beginning.

When they get in the middle of it and they are missing time from work and they are suffering emotionally and physically from their accident and then they have to wait again for negotiations to be complete, it is very common for clients to get testy, frustrated with everyone; with their doctors, with the insurance company and their lawyers. It's just part of the process, part of the game, part of the way of life for the attorney and the client during the unfolding of a personal injury case.

# How Can Someone Expedite A Personal Injury Case?

I would recommend that they follow their doctor's healthcare advice to a T and to absolutely do everything their healthcare providers tell them exactly and fully; don't skip appointments, don't go against medical advice, do everything the doctors tell you, fill every prescription, and go to every

therapy appointment because all of it is good for you and it's good for your case. Follow the attorney's advice to go to all the doctors' appointments because it's in the best interest of them and their claims.

They should follow their attorney's advice about things that we have talked about; not going on social media, acting in the truthful and correct way in their life consistent with their injuries. Don't go out dancing or bowling or riding a bicycle if it's not consistent with your medical condition and medical advice. The attorney will also counsel patience on the part of the client and ask them to not get frustrated, although they will. When it comes to recommending an amount for settlement, there will come a time when the insurance company will say, “That’s it. No more. Take the money we’ve offered or sue us”.

After back and forth negotiations, they should seriously consider following their attorney’s advice when it comes to telling you to accept a settlement because it’s as fair and reasonable as it will get and it will take a year and a half for a trial or, on the other side, they tell you to not accept an offer and go to trial because you can do much better with the judge or a jury.

The simple lesson is, follow your doctor’s advice and follow your lawyer’s advice.

# WHAT MAKES YOUR FIRM A GOOD CHOICE FOR SOMEONE WITH A PERSONAL INJURY CASE?

I have been handling personal injury cases for nearly 30 years; probably several thousand personal injury cases during that time, and they have included almost every kind of personal injury case; motor vehicle accidents, truck accidents, motorcycle accidents, bicycle accidents, slip, trip and falls, dog bites or product liability cases in which a product is defective and injures someone.

We've experienced just about every type of personal injury action that is out there and we have collected millions of dollars in total for our clients over that nearly 30 years. That is the first reason.

The second reason is we give the client a plan of action. We tell them exactly what we have talked about so far, the anatomy of a personal injury case, the way their case will be handled, the direction it will likely go, their responsibility and ours. I am very big on putting a great deal of responsibility for the case on the client because it requires their cooperation with the doctors and their work and their life and they need to know how to handle that, as well as to complete our due diligence and the work necessary to convince the insurance company of the validity and the value of the claim.

That is what I have done and what we collectively have done for nearly 30 years in Northern Virginia.

# DISCLAIMER

This publication is intended to be informational only. No legal advice is being given, and no attorney-client relationship is intended to be created by reading this material. If you are facing legal issues, whether criminal or civil, seek professional legal counsel to get your questions answered.

**NovaLegalGroup, P.C.**

1507 King Street

Alexandria, VA 22314

(703) 548-1462

www.NovaLegalGroup.com

Made in the USA
Monee, IL
05 November 2026

67386566R00055